meet *Emilie Ri...*

Photo by Creation Waits

$\mathcal{N}$ow a USA TODAY bestselling author of women's fiction, Emilie Richards recalls fondly the months she served as a VISTA volunteer in the Arkansas Ozarks.

"This was the country's third poorest county," Emilie said in an interview from her Virginia home. "They had no phones, no safe water supply and no indoor plumbing. But the women created beauty out of nothing—turning scraps of old clothing and feedsacks into exquisitely beautiful quilts."

Emilie said the women insisted she quilt with them in the evenings, "and then later, they'd take out my stitches," she laughingly recalls of her early attempts at the craft.

The 20-year-old college student was left with a richness of experience and a love of quilting that would forever change her life and ultimately inspire a series of novels about the age-old craft. Emilie went on to finish her undergraduate degree in American studies and her master's in family development. She served as a therapist in a mental health center, as a parent services coordinator for Head Start families and in several pastoral counseling centers. Now a full-time writer, Emilie has drawn on these experiences while crafting more than 50 novels.

In *Sister's Choice*, Emilie's fifth and newest Shenandoah Album novel in the popular series, the colorful theme of quilting weaves through the story of a young woman's extraordinary plan to heal her relationship with her sister. Five pattern books, *Quilt Along with Emilie Richards—Wedding Ring, Endless Chain, Lover's Knot, Touching Stars,* and *Sister's Choice*—offer fans a chance to create their own versions of the quilts in her novels.

To learn more about Emilie, visit her Web site at www.emilierichards.com.

LEISURE ARTS. INC.
Little Rock, Arkansas

Read the books that *Inspired* the projects

Leisure Arts is pleased to offer these quilting instruction books as companions to Emilie's compelling Shenandoah Album stories. Each *Quilt Along with Emilie Richards* pattern book includes instructions to create quilts that are featured in the novels. The latest is *Quilt Along with Emilie Richards: Sister's Choice*, offering seven projects as made by Jamie Dunkirk, Alison Dunkirk, Grace Cashel, and the SCC quilters. These include one full-size and two twin-size bed quilts, a throw, and three patterns for baby quilts.

Enhanced with excerpts from the novels, each *Quilt Along with Emilie Richards* book gives the reader a glimpse of the unforgettable characters created by the gifted author.

Now there are five exciting novels in Emilie Richards' *Shenandoah Album* Series, *Wedding Ring, Endless Chain, Lover's Knot, Touching Stars*, and *Sister's Choice*. Each is rich with family drama, romance—and quilts!

Read Emilie Richards' *Shenandoah Album* novels, then quilt along with the good folks of Toms Brook and Fitch Crossing Road. You may just discover a lifelong passion of your very own!

2

Meet the characters from
Sister's Choice

jamie dunkirk

With nine years and a turbulent childhood between them, Kendra and Jamie have never been storybook sisters. After a long estrangement, they've finally begun to forge a new bond. Now Jamie is offering a gift Kendra has long since given up hoping for—a baby. Already raising two young girls on her own, Jamie wants to become a gestational surrogate for Kendra and her husband, Isaac, giving birth to a child the husband and wife have created together. In addition to this amazing gift of life, Jamie has designed a new house for Kendra and Isaac and is overseeing its construction on the Shenandoah River. By giving her sister both a home and a family, Jamie hopes to prove to Kendra that she deserves absolution from her past mistakes.

"Jamie wasn't sure when the idea had taken root, but she had caught an interview on a morning news show with a woman who had carried her infertile sister's baby. She'd felt as if a question had been answered, a miracle had been witnessed. Somewhere inside, she must have nurtured this possibility, even if the words hadn't surfaced. Because when she heard the woman recount the joys of giving her beloved sister a baby she could not bring into the world herself, Jamie had known, beyond the shadow of a doubt, that this was her mission, too."

—from Sister's Choice

kendra taylor

Nine years ago, Jamie ran away from home, leaving older sister Kendra anxious and filled with self-doubt about her efforts to raise Jamie. Since then, Jamie has become a responsible mom herself and is trying to make amends with Kendra by giving her a child of her own. For Kendra, Jamie's offer is like a dream come true—if only she can put the past and all her fears to rest.

cash rosslyn

With his skill at remaining unattached to either a career or a woman, Cash Rosslyn seems to be a country boy who'll never put down roots. However, Jamie learns there's a reason for Cash's cautiousness. And although she certainly isn't looking for a relationship at present, she can't help wondering what he'll think of her plan to be a surrogate mother for Kendra and Isaac's baby.

"Most of the time Kendra Taylor found that spending time with her nieces helped fill an empty space inside her. But there were moments when Kendra found herself wishing she and her husband could enjoy the high-voltage electricity of children in their lives."

—from
Sister's Choice

"Cash was an attractive man. Jamie felt his interest and saw it in his eyes. She reminded herself that she was feeling lonely and was therefore a tad too receptive to the warmth in his smile."
—from Sister's Choice

grace cashel

Grace Cashel is an original. It shows in the art quilts she creates and the outlandish way she dresses. Yet, when she meets Jamie Dunkirk, Grace realizes the quiet young woman is a kindred spirit. Both have faced personal challenges that tested the strength of family bonds. Grace, however, has the advantage of her years. With all the vibrant charm of her personality at her disposal, she assigns herself an exciting new task: Make Jamie a part of her family.

"Granny Grace was willowy and slender, with iron-gray hair and sharp features. Harem pants billowed around her hips and tucked in at her ankles; a hip length vest, sprinkled heavily with crystal beads, sparkled like a fireworks display. She wore gold tennis shoes, and her fingernails were a deep scarlet. Jamie was enchanted. Normally she was suspicious of outrageous women, but Grace had already paid close attention to Jamie's children and made connections."

—from Sister's Choice

Rose of Sharon Quilt

Helen Henry is a prominent member of the Shenandoah Community Church quilting bee. When the senior quilter suggested a Rose of Sharon quilt for the bee's next Christmas project, she may have had in mind a design very much like this vintage quilt. Traditional needle-turn appliqué takes time to do, but many quilters find that the results are well worth the effort. Besides, as Helen knows, the real joy of quilting is the satisfaction of seeing your quilt take shape.

Finished Quilt Size: 86³/₄" x 86³/₄" (220 cm x 220 cm)
Finished Block Size: 24" x 24" (61 cm x 61 cm)

CUTTING OUT THE PIECES

*Follow **Rotary Cutting**, page 50, to cut fabric. Borders include an extra 4" in length for "insurance" and will be trimmed after piecing quilt top center. Cream squares are cut larger than needed and will be trimmed after adding appliqués. Side and corner triangles will be cut from appliquéd large and small squares. All measurements include $^1/_4$" seam allowances.*

From cream solid fabric:
- Cut 2 *lengthwise* **top/bottom borders** $9^1/_2$" x $90^1/_2$".
- Cut 2 *lengthwise* **side borders** $9^1/_2$" x $72^1/_2$".
- Cut 1 **large square** $37^1/_4$" x $37^1/_4$".
- Cut 5 **medium squares** $26^1/_2$" x $26^1/_2$".
- Cut 2 **small squares** $19^7/_8$" x $19^7/_8$".

From green solid fabric:
- Cut 10 *crosswise* **binding strips** $2^1/_8$".
- Cut 1 **square for vine** 23" x 23".

CUTTING OUT THE APPLIQUÉ PIECES

*Follow **Template Cutting**, page 51, to cut appliqué pieces from templates using patterns on pages 11 – 13.*

From green solid fabric:
- Cut 20 **stems a.**
- Cut 20 **stems b.**
- Cut 4 **stems c.**
- Cut 4 **stems d.**
- Cut 4 **stems e.**
- Cut 4 **stems f.**
- Cut 4 **stems g.**
- Cut 4 **stems h.**
- Cut 52 **calyxes v.**
- Cut 20 **calyxes w.**
- Cut 112 **leaves x.**
- Cut 20 **leaves y.**
- Cut 20 **leaves z.**

From red solid fabric:
- Cut 5 **flowers i.**
- Cut 4 **flowers j.**
- Cut 24 **flowers k.**
- Cut 4 **flowers l.**
- Cut 4 **flowers m.**
- Cut 52 **buds n.**
- Cut 20 **buds o.**
- Cut 4 **buds p.**
- Cut 4 **buds q.**

From yellow solid fabric:
- Cut 5 **flower centers r.**
- Cut 24 **flower centers s.**
- Cut 8 **flower centers t.**
- Cut 4 **flower centers u.**

YARDAGE REQUIREMENTS
Yardage is based on 43"/44" (109 cm/112 cm) wide fabric.

$8^3/_8$ yds (7.7 m) of cream solid fabric

$3^7/_8$ yds (3.5 m) of green solid fabric (includes binding)

$1^1/_4$ yds (1.1 m) of red solid fabric

$^1/_4$ yd (23 cm) of yellow solid fabric

8 yds (7.3 m) of fabric for backing

You will also need:
95" x 95" (241 cm x 241 cm) piece of batting

Template plastic

Water-soluble fabric marking pen

Block
(make 5)

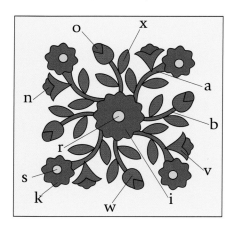

Fig. 1

Fig. 2

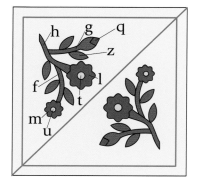

ADDING THE APPLIQUÉS

Follow Needle-Turn Appliqué, page 54, to add appliqués in order listed below.

1. To make **Block**, arrange and appliqué the pieces listed below on 1 cream solid **medium square**. Centering design, trim **Block** to 24¹/₂" x 24¹/₂". Make 5 **Blocks**.
    4 **stems a**
    4 **stems b**
    1 **flower i**
    4 **flowers k**
    1 **flower center r**
    4 **flower centers s**
    4 **buds n**
    4 **buds o**
    4 **calyxes v**
    4 **calyxes w**
    16 **leaves x**

2. For **Side Triangles**, use fabric marking pen to draw 2 diagonal lines (corner to corner) across cream solid **large square**. Draw line around **large square** 1" from raw edges. Arrange and appliqué the pieces listed below on *each* drawn triangle (**Fig. 1**). Cut along outer drawn line to trim **large square** and then cut along diagonal lines to make 4 **Side Triangles**.
    1 **bud p**
    1 **stem c**
    1 **stem d**
    1 **stem e**
    1 **flower j**
    1 **flower k**
    1 **flower center s**
    1 **flower center t**
    5 **leaves y**

3. For **Corner Triangles**, use fabric marking pen to draw 1 diagonal line (corner to corner) across 1 cream solid **small square**. Draw line around **small square** 1" from raw edges. Arrange and appliqué the pieces listed below on *each* drawn triangle (**Fig. 2**). Cut along outer drawn line to trim **small square** and then cut along diagonal line to make 2 **Corner Triangles**. Repeat with remaining **small square** to make a *total* of 4 **Corner Triangles**.
    1 **bud q**
    1 **stem f**
    1 **stem g**
    1 **stem h**
    1 **flower l**
    1 **flower m**
    1 **flower center t**
    1 **flower center u**
    5 **leaves z**

ASSEMBLING THE QUILT TOP CENTER

Follow **Piecing**, *page 51, and* **Pressing**, *page 53, to assemble quilt top center. Refer to* **Assembly Diagram** *for placement.*

1. Sew **Blocks**, **Side Triangles** and **Corner Triangles** together into diagonal **Rows**.
2. Sew **Rows** together and then add remaining **Corner Triangles** to make **Quilt Top Center**.

ADDING THE BORDERS

Refer to photo, page 10, for placement.

1. To determine length of **side borders**, measure *length* of **Quilt Top Center** through center of quilt. Trim **side borders** to determined length.
2. Matching centers and corners, sew **side borders** to **Quilt Top Center**.
3. To determine length of **top/bottom borders**, measure *width* of **Quilt Top** through center of quilt, including added borders. Trim **top/bottom borders** to determined length.
4. Matching centers and corners, sew **top/bottom borders** to **Quilt Top**.
5. For vine, use **square for vine** and follow **Making a Continuous Bias Strip**, page 59, to make approximately 9$^1/_2$ yds of 1$^1/_4$"w bias strip. Press long edges of bias strip $^1/_4$" to wrong side to make vine.
6. Arrange vine on borders. Arrange 32 *each* of **buds n**, **calyxes v**, and **leaves x** along vine. Follow **Needle-Turn Appliqué**, page 54, to appliqué vine and appliqué pieces to quilt top.

Assembly Diagram

"'*Oh*, will you look at this?' Grace said. Just ahead of her, draped in a large round hoop, was what looked to be a queen-size quilt. 'Why, Helen, it's spectacular. Whig Rose?'

'No. Rose of Sharon. See the way the stems bend? Some folks claim that's the difference, but a quilt's a quilt by any name, isn't it?'"

—from Sister's Choice

9

COMPLETING THE QUILT

1. Follow **Quilting**, page 54, to mark, layer, and quilt as desired. Our quilt is channel quilted by hand. The background is channel quilted with vertical lines in the blocks, horizontal lines in the triangles, and diagonal lines in the border. The corners of the quilt top are crosshatch quilted.
2. Follow **Binding**, page 60, and use **binding strips** to bind quilt.

"The quilt was gorgeous. Grace counted five blocks set on point so they looked like diamonds, each one with a red flower in the center and curving stems radiating outward. Each stem was adorned with either flowers or buds, and sometimes both. The border was particularly lovely, a sinuous vine that went all the way around the quilt. It, too, was adorned with small red buds."

—from Sister's Choice

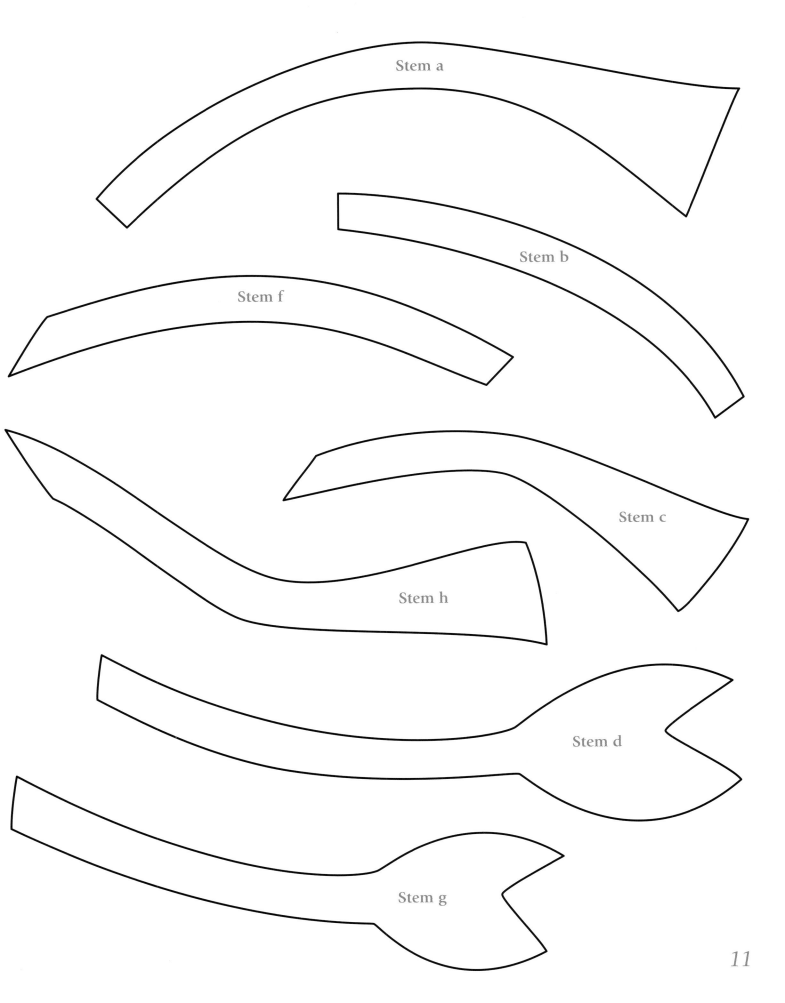

Stem a

Stem b

Stem f

Stem c

Stem h

Stem d

Stem g

Flower i

Flower k

Flower m

Bud o

Bud n

Calyx w

Stem e

Center r

Center s

Leaf y

Center t

Center
u

Bud p

Bud q

Leaf z

Leaf x

Flower j

Flower l

Calyx v

13

Snake in the Hollow Quilt

A few years ago, Reese Claiborne's parents moved in with Helen Henry to keep an eye on her and help care for her old farmhouse. At the time, Helen chose to think they were just staying with her until they could get a place of their own, but Reese quickly captured Helen's heart. It won't be a surprise to anyone if this colorful quilt is just one of many Helen will create for Reese.

Finished Quilt Size: 70³/₄" x 90³/₄" (180 cm x 231 cm)
Finished Block Size: 10" x 10" (25 cm x 25 cm)

CUTTING OUT THE PIECES

*Follow **Template Cutting**, page 51, and use patterns on page 19, to cut fabric using templates. Follow **Rotary Cutting**, page 50, to cut borders and binding strips. Borders include an extra 4" in length for "insurance" and will be trimmed after piecing quilt top center. All measurements include $^1/_4$" seam allowances.*

From light green print fabric:
- Cut 9 *crosswise* **binding strips** $2^1/_8$"w.
- Cut 2 *lengthwise* **side borders** $5^1/_2$" x $84^1/_2$".
- Cut 2 *lengthwise* **top/bottom borders** $5^1/_2$" x $74^1/_2$".
- Cut 48 **A's**.

From assorted bright print fabrics:
- Cut 96 **B's**.
- Cut 576 **C's**.

YARDAGE REQUIREMENTS

Yardage is based on 43"/44" (109 cm/112 cm) wide fabric.

$5^5/_8$ yds (5.1 m) of light green print fabric (includes binding)

$5^3/_4$ yds (5.3 m) *total* of assorted bright print fabrics

$5^1/_2$ yds (5 m) of fabric for backing

You will also need: 79" x 99" (201 cm x 251 cm) piece of batting

Template plastic

"Show-and-tell continued around the circle and stopped at Helen. She unfolded what looked to be a twin-size quilt.

'Little Reese Claiborne is awful fond of snakes, which concerns me no end, just the way you'd expect. Anyway, I decided to make her a snake-in-the hollow quilt. And that girl likes bright colors, so that's what she's getting.'"

—from Sister's Choice

Unit 1
(make 96)

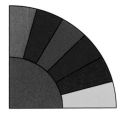

Unit 2
(make 96)

Block
(make 48)

MAKING THE BLOCKS

*Follow **Piecing**, page 51, and **Pressing**, page 53, to make blocks. Use ¹/₄" seam allowances throughout.*

1. Sew 6 **C**'s together to make **Unit 1**. Make 96 **Unit 1**'s.
2. *(**Note:** To sew curved seams in Steps 2 and 3, pin at center and at each end, then add additional pins as needed.)* With **Unit 1** on top, sew 1 **Unit 1** and 1 **B** together to make **Unit 2**. Make 96 **Unit 2**'s.
3. With **A** on top, sew 1 **Unit 2** to each side of 1 **A** to make **Block**. Make 48 **Blocks**.

ASSEMBLING THE QUILT TOP CENTER

*Refer to **Quilt Top Diagram**, page 17, for placement.*

1. Sew 6 **Blocks** together to make 1 **Row**. Make 8 **Rows**.
2. Sew **Rows** together to make **Quilt Top Center**.

ADDING THE BORDERS

1. To determine length of **side borders**, measure *length* of **Quilt Top Center** through center. Trim **side borders** to determined length.
2. Matching centers and corners, sew **side borders** to **Quilt Top Center**.
3. To determine length of **top/bottom borders**, measure *width* of **Quilt Top** through center, including added borders. Trim **top/bottom borders** to determined length.
4. Matching centers and corners, sew **top/bottom borders** to **Quilt Top**.

COMPLETING THE QUILT

1. Follow **Quilting**, page 54, to mark, layer, and quilt as desired. Our quilt is machine quilted with a zigzag pattern in the large pieced curves made by pieces C and flowers in pieces A and B. The border has a continuous loop, leaf, and flower pattern.
2. Follow **Binding**, page 60, and use **binding strips** to bind quilt.

Quilt Top Diagram

"Jewel-toned snakes slithered across a pale green background. The quilt was made of fan blocks with a fan in opposing corners of each block. When set together, the fans did indeed look like snakes side-winding their way across the quilt. Helen's placement of colors and her use of many child-pleasing prints set this quilt apart. Any child worth her salt would adore it."

—from Sister's Choice

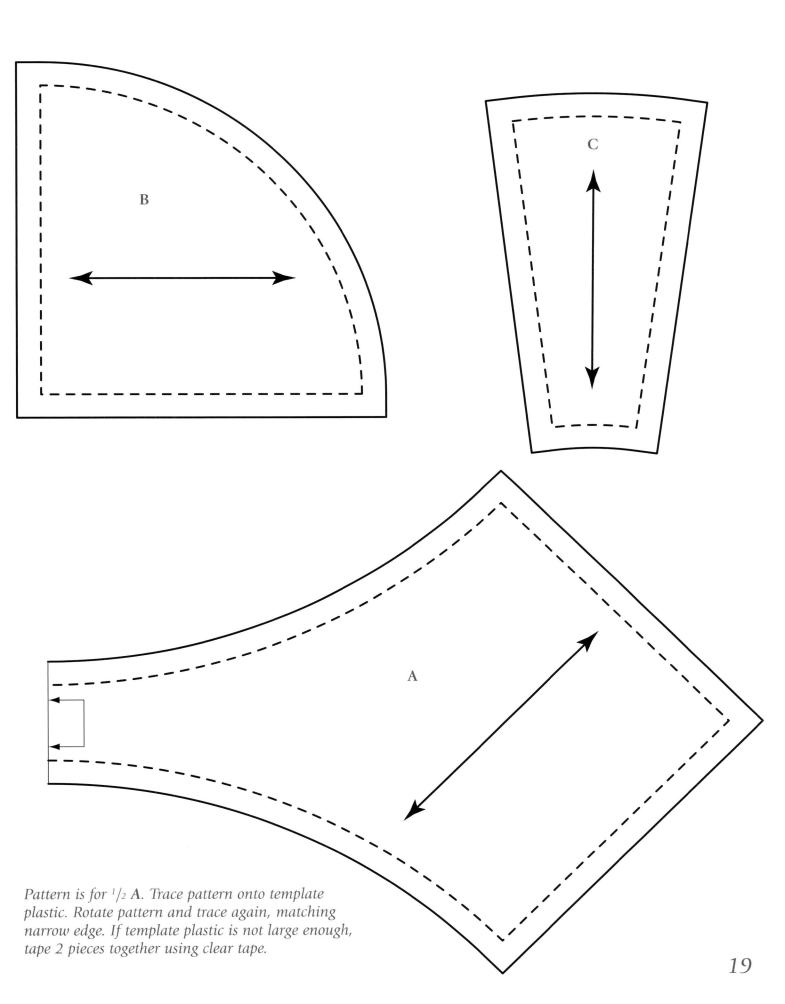

B

C

A

Pattern is for ¹/₂ **A**. Trace pattern onto template plastic. Rotate pattern and trace again, matching narrow edge. If template plastic is not large enough, tape 2 pieces together using clear tape.

19

Alison's First Quilt

Grace has volunteered to help Jamie's daughters, Hannah and Alison, make their first quilts. For Alison's quilt, Grace helped the four-year-old choose a variety of blue fabrics from her own quilting stash so she could sew and tie a pretty blanket like this one. Four-Patch blocks, Framed Square blocks, and plain setting squares make this pattern truly simple to sew.

Finished Quilt Size: 70³/₄" x 90³/₄" (180 cm x 231 cm)
Finished Block Size: 10" x 10" (25 cm x 25 cm)

"'I like blue!' Alison shouted. 'Very, very, very blue! Like the sky. Like stars.'"

—from Sister's Choice

CUTTING OUT THE PIECES

*Follow **Rotary Cutting**, page 50, to cut fabric. All measurements include 1/4" seam allowances.*

For *each* Block A
- Cut 1 **large square** 10¹/₂" x 10¹/₂".

For *each* Block B
- Cut 2 light blue print **small squares** 5¹/₂" x 5¹/₂".
- Cut 2 dark blue print **small squares** 5¹/₂" x 5¹/₂".

For *each* Block C
- Cut 1 dark blue **small square** 5¹/₂" x 5¹/₂".
- From 1 light blue print, cut 2 **small rectangles** 3" x 5¹/₂" and 2 **large rectangles** 3" x 10¹/₂".

For *each* Block D
- Cut 1 light blue **small square** 5¹/₂" x 5¹/₂".
- From 1 dark blue print, cut 2 **small rectangles** 3" x 5¹/₂" and 2 **large rectangles** 3" x 10¹/₂".

From fabric for binding:
- Cut 9 *crosswise* **binding strips** 2¹/₈"w.

Use any number of prints and make any variety of Blocks for your quilt. When choosing your prints, about half should be "light" and the other half "dark." You will need a total of 63 Blocks, but you may wish to make a few extras for more options when arranging your quilt.

YARDAGE REQUIREMENTS

Yardage is based on 43"/44" (109 cm/112 cm) wide fabric and should be generous to cut required number of Blocks in any combination desired.

7¹/₈ yds (6.5 m) *total* of assorted light and dark blue print fabrics

5¹/₂ yds (5 m) fabric for backing

⁵/₈ yd (57 cm) fabric for binding

You will also need: 79" x 99" (201 cm x 251 cm) piece of batting

White size 3 pearl cotton (optional)

Block B

Unit 1

Block C

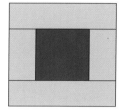

Block D

MAKING THE BLOCKS

*Follow **Piecing**, page 51, and **Pressing**, page 53, to make blocks. Use ¹/₄" seam allowances throughout.*

1. Sew 2 light blue print **small squares** and 2 dark blue print **small squares** together to make **Block B**.
2. Sew 2 light blue print **small rectangles** and 1 dark blue print **small square** together to make **Unit 1**.
3. Sew 2 light blue print **large rectangles** and 1 **Unit 1** together to make **Block C**.
4. Repeat Steps 2 and 3 using 1 light blue print **small square**, 2 dark blue print **small rectangles,** and 2 dark blue print **large rectangles** to make **Block D**.
5. Make a *total* of 63 **Blocks** in desired combination.

ASSEMBLING THE QUILT TOP

1. On floor or other large flat surface, arrange **Blocks** into 9 **Rows** of 7 **Blocks** each to determine desired placement. Refer to photo as a suggestion.
2. Sew **Blocks** together into **Rows**.
3. Sew **Rows** together to make **Quilt Top**.

COMPLETING THE QUILT

1. Follow **Tying a Quilt**, page 58, to tie quilt, or follow **Quilting**, page 54, to mark, layer, and quilt as desired. Our quilt is tied at corners where blocks meet using white size 3 pearl cotton.
2. Follow **Binding**, page 60, and use **binding strips** to bind quilt.

Sister's Choice Quilt

*W*anting to do something special for Kendra and Isaac's child, while also being curious to learn if she will like quilt-making, Jamie decides to make a baby quilt. Since she thoroughly enjoys shopping for the fabrics, her future as a quilter does seem to be bright. Jamie learns this time-honored pattern is the same one Grace used for her first quilt—and it's a fascinating story that she reveals to Jamie as they stitch together.

Finished Quilt Size: 50³/₄" x 50³/₄" (129 cm x 129 cm)
Finished Block Size: 10" x 10" (25 cm x 25 cm)

YARDAGE REQUIREMENTS

Yardage is based on 43"/44" (109 cm/112 cm) wide fabric.

$1^1/_2$ yds (1.4 m) of cream print fabric

$^5/_8$ yd (57 cm) of black print fabric

2 yds (1.8 m) red print fabric (includes binding)

$3^3/_8$ yds (3.1 m) of fabric for backing

You will also need:
59" x 59"
(150 cm x 150 cm)
piece of batting

CUTTING OUT THE PIECES

*Follow **Rotary Cutting**, page 50, to cut fabric. Cut all strips across the selvage-to-selvage width of the fabric unless otherwise indicated. Cutting lengths for borders are exact. All measurements include $^1/_4$" seam allowances. **Note:** Colors for alternate color way quilt shown on page 28 are listed in parentheses.*

From cream print fabric:
- Cut 11 **strips** $2^1/_2$" x 20". (Yellow)
- Cut 2 **top/bottom inner borders** $1^1/_2$" x $42^1/_2$", pieced as needed. (White)
- Cut 2 **side inner borders** $1^1/_2$" x $40^1/_2$", pieced as needed. (White)
- Cut 5 strips $2^7/_8$" wide. From these strips, cut 64 **large squares** $2^7/_8$" x $2^7/_8$". (White)
- Cut 4 strips $2^1/_2$" wide. From these strips, cut 64 **small squares** $2^1/_2$" x $2^1/_2$". (Yellow)

From black print fabric:
- Cut 5 strips $2^7/_8$" wide. From these strips, cut 64 **large squares** $2^7/_8$" x $2^7/_8$". (Green–Cut **outer borders** first.)
- Cut 3 **strips** $2^1/_2$" x 20". (Orange)

From red print fabric:
- Cut 6 **binding strips** $2^1/_8$"w. (Green)
- Cut 2 *lengthwise* **top/bottom outer borders** $4^1/_2$" x $50^1/_2$". (Green)
- Cut 2 *lengthwise* **side outer borders** $4^1/_2$" x $42^1/_2$". (Green)
  From remaining width, cut:
- Cut 8 strips $2^1/_2$" wide. From these strips, cut 64 **small squares** $2^1/_2$" x $2^1/_2$". (Orange)
- Cut 10 **strips** $2^1/_2$" x 20". (Green)

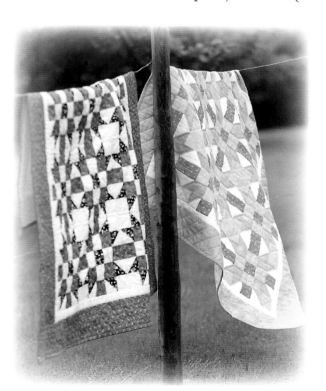

"'There's a pattern, an old traditional pattern, called Sister's Choice,' said Grace. 'Doesn't that seem appropriate to your situation?'"

—from Sister's Choice

MAKING THE SISTER'S CHOICE BLOCKS

Follow Piecing, page 51, and Pressing, page 53, to make blocks. Use ¹/₄" seam allowances throughout.

1. Draw a diagonal line on wrong side of each cream (white) print **large square**.

2. Matching right sides, place 1 cream (white) print **large square** on top of 1 black (green) print **large square**. Referring to **Fig. 1**, stitch ¹/₄" from each side of drawn line; cut along drawn line. Press open to make 2 **Triangle-Squares**. Make 128 **Triangle-Squares**.

3. Sew 2 red (green) print **strips** and 1 cream (yellow) print **strip** together to make **Strip Set A**. Press seam allowances toward red (green) strips. Make 5 **Strip Set A's**. Cut **Strip Set A's** at 2¹/₂" intervals to make 32 **Unit 1's**.

4. Sew 2 cream (yellow) print **strips** and 1 black (orange) print **strip** together to make **Strip Set B**. Press seam allowances toward black (orange) strip. Make 3 **Strip Set B's**. Cut **Strip Set B's** at 2¹/₂" intervals to make 16 **Unit 2's**.

5. Sew 2 **Unit 1's** and 1 **Unit 2** together to make **Unit 3**. Make 16 **Unit 3's**.

6. Sew 2 **Triangle-Squares** and 1 red (orange) print **small square** together to make **Unit 4**. Make 64 **Unit 4's**.

7. Sew 2 **Unit 4's** and 1 **Unit 3** together to make **Unit 5**. Make 16 **Unit 5's**.

Fig. 1

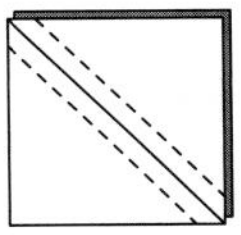

Triangle-Squares
(make 128)

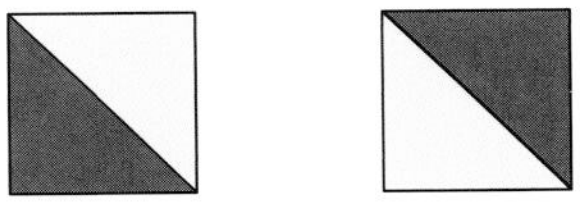

Strip Set A
(make 5)

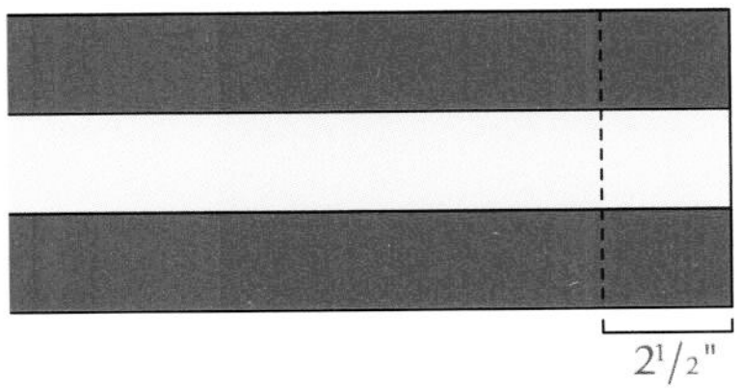

2¹/₂"

Unit 1
(make 32)

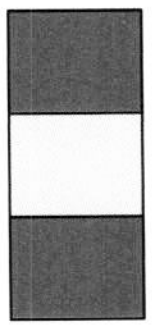

Strip Set B
(make 3)

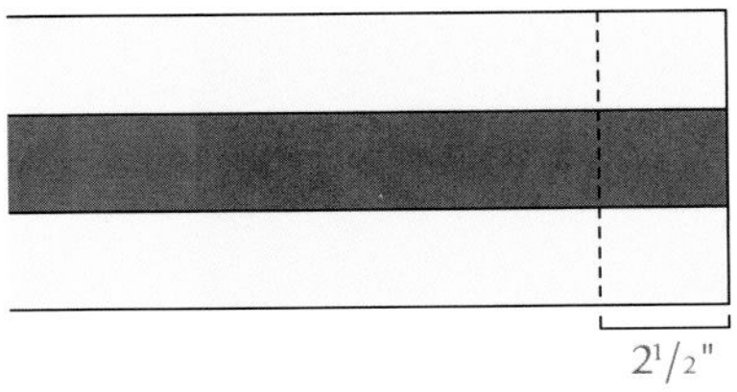

2¹/₂"

Unit 2
(make 16)

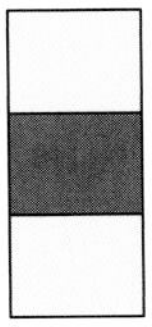

Unit 3
(make 16)

Unit 4
(make 64)

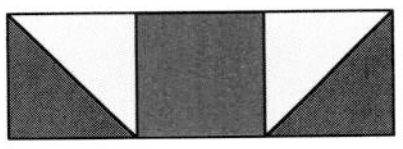

Unit 5
(make 16)

Unit 6
(make 32)

Block
(make 16)

8. Sew 2 cream (yellow) print **small squares** and 1 **Unit 4** together to make **Unit 6**. Make 32 **Unit 6's**.
9. Sew 2 **Unit 6's** and 1 **Unit 5** together to make **Block**. Make 16 **Blocks**.

ASSEMBLING THE QUILT TOP CENTER
*Refer to **Quilt Top Diagram** for placement.*
1. Sew 4 **Blocks** together to make 1 **Row**. Make 4 **Rows**.
2. Sew **Rows** together to make **Quilt Top Center**.

ADDING THE BORDERS
1. Matching centers and corners, sew **side inner borders** to **Quilt Top Center**.
2. Matching centers and corners, sew **top/bottom inner borders** to **Quilt Top**.
3. Repeat Steps 1 – 2 to add **side**, then **top/bottom outer borders** to **Quilt Top**.

COMPLETING THE QUILT
1. Follow **Quilting**, page 54, to mark, layer, and quilt as desired. Our quilt is machine quilted with outline quilting in the black triangles and cream corner squares of the blocks, curved quilting in the red and black squares of the nine-patches, and a continuous loop and bone pattern in the outer border.
2. Follow **Making a Hanging Sleeve**, page 59, if a hanging sleeve is desired.
3. Follow **Binding**, page 60, and use **binding strips** to bind quilt.

Quilt Top Diagram

"Jamie had shopped for hours online and at two different quilt shops until she found what she wanted. She had chosen three fabrics: Black with the white silhouettes of puppies and kittens, white with tiny red umbrellas and yellow ducklings in rain slickers, and finally bright red with cheerful one-word inscriptions such as 'love' and 'kindness' and 'laughter' printed in white and black. The fabric made her smile, and the Sister's Choice design was graphic enough to show it to perfection."

—from Sister's Choice

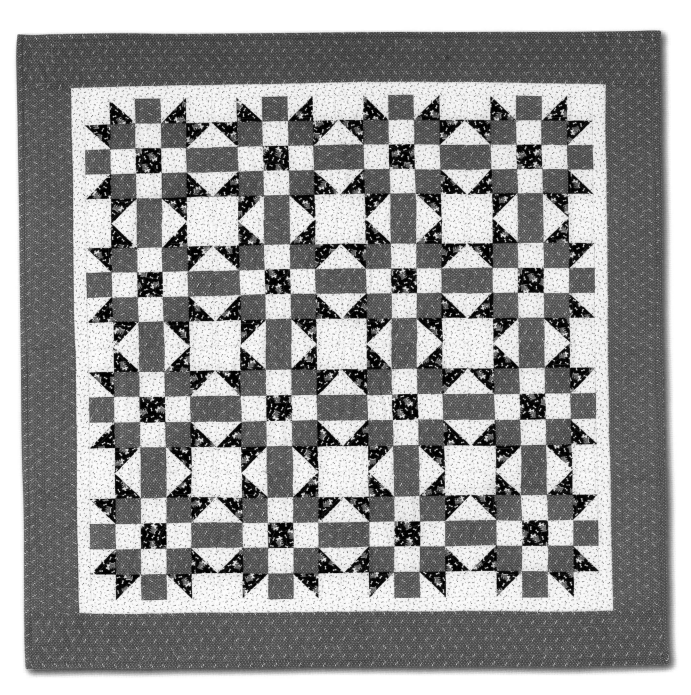

Sister's Choice Quilt
Alternate Color Way

*O*ne reason Grace is fond of the Sister's Choice block is that the simple shapes take on an altogether different look when the color values change. This little quilt uses four fabrics, where Jamie's red quilt, made from the same pattern, uses only three.

This color way requires:
3/4 yd (69 cm) of white solid fabric
1/2 yd (46 cm) of orange print fabric
7/8 yd (80 cm) of yellow print fabric
2 1/8 yds (1.9 m) of green print fabric (includes binding)
3 3/8 yds (3.1 m) of fabric for backing

Instructions are found on pages 24 – 26.

Bear's Paw Quilt

Some of the most interesting quilts are the ones inspired by—other quilts! For instance, this teddy bear baby quilt, complete with Bear's Paw blocks and embroidered squares, is based on the Bee's bazaar quilt and SCC Bee member Kate Brogan's redwork embroidery.

Finished Quilt Size: 44^1/$_4$" x 44^1/$_4$" (112 cm x 112 cm)
Finished Block Size: 10^1/$_2$" x 10^1/$_2$" (27 cm x 27 cm)

YARDAGE REQUIREMENTS

Yardage is based on 43"/44" (109 cm/112 cm) wide fabric.

7/8 yd (80 cm) of white solid fabric

3/8 yd (34 cm) of white print fabric #1

3/4 yd (69 cm) of white print fabric #2

1/4 yd (23 cm) of red print fabric #1

1 1/4 yds (1.1 m) red print fabric #2 (includes binding)

2 3/4 yds (2.5 m) of fabric for backing

You will also need:
49" x 49" (124 cm x 124 cm) piece of batting

Fine-point water-soluble fabric marking pen

Red embroidery floss

Note: We recommend setting the floss color before stitching by soaking floss in a mixture of 1 tablespoon vinegar and 1 cup water. Allow floss to air dry.

CUTTING OUT THE PIECES

*Follow **Rotary Cutting**, page 50, to cut fabric. Cut all strips across the selvage-to-selvage width of the fabric. Cutting lengths for borders are exact. All measurements include 1/4" seam allowances.*

From white solid fabric:
- Cut 2 strips 13" wide. From these strips, cut 4 **large squares** 13" x 13".

From white print fabric #1:
- Cut 3 strips 2 3/8" wide. From these strips, cut 40 **small squares** 2 3/8" x 2 3/8".
- Cut 1 strip 2" wide. From this strip, cut 20 **smallest squares** 2" x 2".

From white print fabric #2:
- Cut 3 strips 2" wide. From these strips, cut 20 **rectangles** 2" x 5".
- Cut 8 strips 2" wide. From these strips, cut 24 **sashings** 2" x 11".

From red print fabric #1:
- Cut 2 strips 3 1/2" wide. From these strips, cut 20 **medium squares** 3 1/2" x 3 1/2".

From red print fabric #2:
- Cut 3 strips 2 3/8" wide. From these strips, cut 40 **small squares** 2 3/8" x 2 3/8".
- Cut 2 strips 2" wide. From these strips, cut 21 **smallest squares** 2" x 2".
- Cut 2 **side borders** 3 1/2" x 38".
- Cut 2 **top/bottom borders** 3 1/2" x 44", pieced as needed.
- Cut 5 **binding strips** 2 1/8"w.

"'We have our bear's paw quilt in the frame for our fall bazaar,' said Cathy Adams, the chairman of the Shenandoah Community Church Bee. 'And I know some of you brought your own projects to work on. First, though, we'll have show-and-tell. If you have something that you're in the midst of, hold that up and tell us what it is.'

Kate Brogan pulled out a nursery-rhyme block she was embroidering in red embroidery floss and held it up."

—from Sister's Choice

MAKING THE EMBROIDERED BLOCKS

*Embroidery patterns are on pages 33 – 36. Embroidery stitches listed are included in **Hand Stitches**, page 62.*

1. Referring to **Quilt Top Diagram**, page 32, trace embroidery patterns onto **large squares** by placing **large squares** over patterns and using water-soluble fabric marking pen.
2. Use 3 strands of floss for all stitching. Work Stem Stitches for bear outlines, Satin Stitches for eyes and noses, Back Stitches for words, and French Knots for dots.
3. Centering design, trim each **large square** to 11" x 11" to complete **Embroidered Blocks**.

MAKING THE BEAR'S PAW BLOCKS

*Follow **Piecing**, page 51, and **Pressing**, page 53, to make blocks. Use ¹/₄" seam allowances throughout.*

1. Draw a diagonal line on wrong side of each white print #1 **small square**.
2. Matching right sides, place 1 white print #1 **small square** on top of 1 red print #2 **small square**. Referring to **Fig. 1**, stitch ¹/₄" from each side of drawn line; cut along drawn line. Press open to make 2 **Triangle-Squares**. Make 80 **Triangle-Squares**.
3. Sew 2 **Triangle-Squares** together to make **Unit 1**. Make 20 **Unit 1's**.
4. Sew 2 **Triangle-Squares** and 1 white print fabric #1 **smallest square** together to make **Unit 2**. Make 20 **Unit 2's**.
5. Sew 1 **Unit 1** and 1 red print #1 **medium square** together to make **Unit 3**. Make 20 **Unit 3's**.
6. Sew 1 **Unit 2** and 1 **Unit 3** together to make **Unit 4**. Make 20 **Unit 4's**.
7. Sew 2 **Unit 4's** and 1 white print #2 **rectangle** together to make **Unit 5**. Make 10 **Unit 5's**.
8. Sew 2 white print #2 **rectangles** and 1 red print #2 **smallest square** together to make **Unit 6**. Make 5 **Unit 6's**.
9. Sew 2 **Unit 5's** and 1 **Unit 6** together to make **Bear's Paw Block**. Make 5 **Bear's Paw Blocks**.

Fig. 1

Triangle-Square
(make 80)

Unit 1
(make 20)

Unit 2
(make 20)

Unit 3
(make 20)

Unit 4
(make 20)

Unit 5
(make 10)

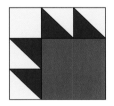

Unit 6
(make 5)

Bear's Paw Block
(make 5)

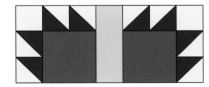

31

ASSEMBLING THE QUILT TOP CENTER
*Refer to **Quilt Top Diagram** for placement.*

1. Sew 4 **sashings**, 2 **Bear's Paw Blocks** and 1 **Embroidered Block** together to make **Row A**. Make 2 **Row A's**.
2. Sew 4 **sashings**, 2 **Embroidered Blocks** and 1 **Bear's Paw Block** together to make **Row B**.
3. Sew 4 red print #2 **smallest squares** and 3 **sashings** together to make **Sashing Row**. Make 4 **Sashing Rows**.
4. Sew **Rows** together to make **Quilt Top Center**.

ADDING THE BORDERS
1. Matching centers and corners, sew **side borders** to **Quilt Top Center**.
2. Matching centers and corners, sew **top/bottom borders** to **Quilt Top**.

COMPLETING THE QUILT
1. Follow **Quilting**, page 54, to mark, layer, and quilt as desired. Our quilt is machine quilted in the ditch around the blocks and "paws."
2. Follow **Making a Hanging Sleeve**, page 59, if a hanging sleeve is desired.
3. Follow **Binding**, page 60, and use **binding strip**s to bind quilt.

Quilt Top Diagram

"Kendra stepped into the small bedroom that looked over the backyard. When Hanna and Alison visited, they slept on twin beds. A fluffy white rug and cheerful redwork quilts she had bought at the Shenandoah Community Church auction harmonized with pale yellow walls."

—from Sister's Choice

Teddy
Bear, 
you are
cuddly,

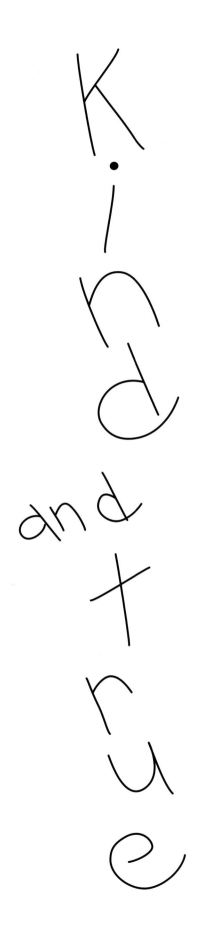

Kind and true

just remember . . .

Crazy Cats Quilt

*O*nce the SCC Bee quilters agree on a project, it fairly puts itself together! Of course, paper piecing also helps speed the process. Most crazy quilts have an unstructured appearance, but the quilters decided to feature a cat print fabric at the center of all their blocks, giving this quilt a playful theme.

Finished Quilt Size: 34³/₄" x 41¹/₄" (88 cm x 105 cm)
Finished Block Size: 6¹/₂" x 6¹/₂" (17 cm x 17 cm)

YARDAGE REQUIREMENTS

Yardage is based on 43"/44" (109 cm/112 cm) wide fabric.

1 yd (91 cm) of novelty print fabric*

1⅞ yds (1.7 m) *total* of assorted print fabrics

¼ yd (23 cm) of pink stripe fabric

⅞ yd (80 cm) of turquoise print fabric (includes binding)

1¼ yds (1.1 m) of fabric for backing

You will also need:
39" x 45" (99 cm x 114 cm) piece of batting

Dark purple embroidery floss

Note: *We recommend setting the floss color before stitching by soaking floss in a mixture of 1 tablespoon vinegar and 1 cup water. Allow floss to air dry.*

*Yardage may vary depending on size and repeat of design.

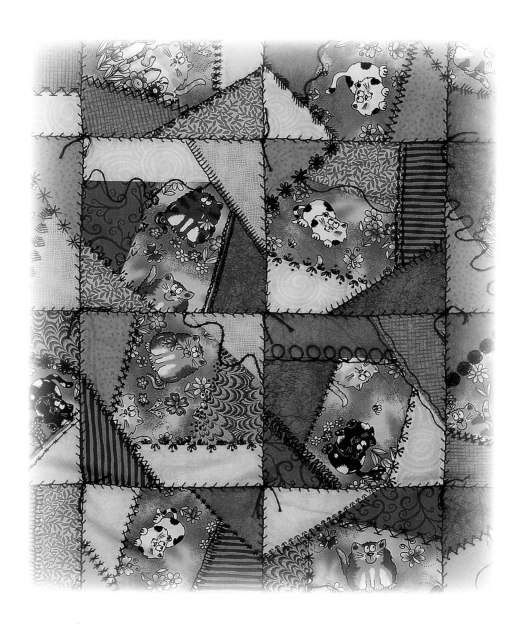

CUTTING OUT THE PIECES

*Follow **Rotary Cutting**, page 50, to cut fabric. Cut all strips across the selvage-to-selvage width of the fabric. Cutting lengths for borders are exact. All measurements include ¼" seam allowances.*

From pink stripe fabric:
- Cut 2 **side inner borders** 1¼" x 33".
- Cut 2 **top/bottom inner borders** 1¼" x 28".

From turquoise print fabric:
- Cut 4 **outer borders** 3¾" x 34½".
- Cut 5 **binding strips** 2⅛"w.

PAPER PIECING THE BLOCKS

Photocopy 20 copies of paper piecing Block Pattern, page 40. Follow Paper Piecing, page 52, to paper piece Blocks.

1. Using **Block Pattern**, center desired motif of novelty fabric over area 1. Use assorted print fabrics in random color order to finish paper piecing **Block**. Randomly rotating novelty motifs, make 20 **Blocks**.

ASSEMBLING THE QUILT TOP CENTER

Follow Piecing, page 51, and Pressing, page 53. Use ¹/₄" seam allowances throughout. Refer to Quilt Top Diagram for placement.

1. Randomly rotating **Blocks**, sew 4 **Blocks** together to make **Row**. Make 5 **Rows**.
2. Sew **Rows** together to make **Quilt Top Center**.
3. Carefully remove paper from **Blocks**.

ADDING THE BORDERS

1. Matching centers and corners, sew **side inner borders** to **Quilt Top Center**.
2. Matching centers and corners, sew **top/bottom inner borders** to **Quilt Top**.
3. Follow Steps 1 – 2 to sew **side** and then **top/bottom outer borders** to **Quilt Top**.

ADDING THE EMBROIDERY

Embroidery stitches are included in Hand Stitches, page 62. Use 3 strands of floss for all embroidery.

1. Work Feather Stitches along seamlines between **Blocks**.
2. Work desired stitches or stitch combinations along seamlines within **Blocks**. Refer to photo, page 38, for suggestions.

COMPLETING THE QUILT

1. Follow **Tying a Quilt**, page 58, to tie quilt at corners where blocks meet using 6 strands of floss.
2. Follow **Making a Hanging Sleeve**, page 59, if a hanging sleeve is desired.
3. Follow **Binding**, page 60, and use **binding strips** and to bind quilt.

Block
(make 20)

Quilt Top Diagram

"Although some people purposely ignored the pregnancy, as if it were a missing nose or ear at which they were afraid to be caught staring, others found ways of showing quiet support. The bee had begun work on a large crazy quilt made from different types of fabrics so that a baby could lie on the floor and investigate with tiny fingers."

—from Sister's Choice

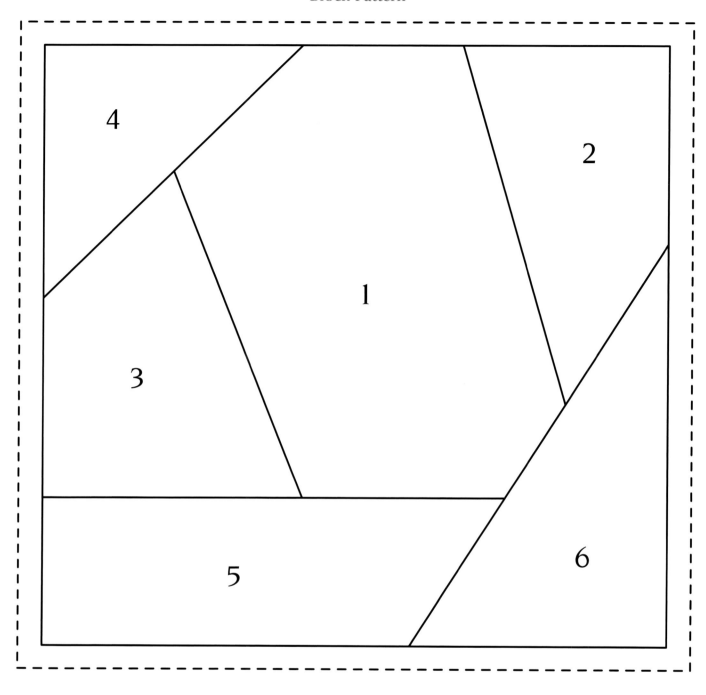

4

2

1

3

6

5

Shining Hour Quilt

Jamie knows that making new friends in Toms Brook will help ease her young daughters' transition from their former home. However, as a surrogate mother to her sister's baby, Jamie herself is bound to become the object of speculation. Grace, who only recently returned to Toms Brook after decades away, joins Jamie as they attend a meeting of the SCC Bee. Both of the new arrivals hope they'll find a warm welcome, as well as inspiration for lovely quilts like this Shining Hour design.

Finished Quilt Size: 48³/₄" x 48³/₄" (124 cm x 124 cm)
Finished Block Size: 12" x 12" (30 cm x 30 cm)

YARDAGE REQUIREMENTS

Yardage is based on 43"/44" (109 cm/112 cm) wide fabric.

$3^3/_8$ yds (3.1 m) of cream polka dot fabric (includes binding)

$1^1/_4$ yds (1.1 m) of pink print fabric

$5/_8$ yd (57 cm) of green print fabric

$1^7/_8$ yd (1.7 m) of blue print fabric

$3^1/_4$ yds (3 m) of fabric for backing

You will also need: 57 x 57" (145 cm x 145 cm) piece of batting

CUTTING OUT THE PIECES

*Follow **Rotary Cutting**, page 50, to cut fabric. Cut all strips across the selvage-to-selvage width of the fabric unless otherwise noted. Cutting lengths for borders are exact. All measurements include $^1/_4$" seam allowances.*

From cream polka dot fabric:
- Cut 6 **binding strips** $2^1/_8$"w.
- Cut 2 *lengthwise* **top/bottom outer borders** 2" x $48^1/_2$".
- Cut 2 *lengthwise* **side outer borders** 2" x $45^1/_2$".
- Cut 2 *lengthwise* **top/bottom inner borders** 2" x $39^1/_2$".
- Cut 2 *lengthwise* **side inner borders** 2" x $36^1/_2$".

From remaining width:
- Cut 3 strips $4^1/_4$"w. From these strips, cut 14 **large squares** $4^1/_4$" x $4^1/_4$".
- Cut 10 strips 2"w. From these strips, cut 112 **small squares** 2" x 2".

From pink print fabric:
- Cut 2 strips $3^1/_2$" wide. From these strips, cut 20 **medium squares** $3^1/_2$" x $3^1/_2$".

From green print fabric:
- Cut 1 strip $3^1/_2$" wide. From this strip, cut 8 **medium squares** $3^1/_2$" x $3^1/_2$".

From blue print fabric:
- Cut 2 strips $4^1/_4$"w. From these strips, cut 14 **large squares** $4^1/_4$" x $4^1/_4$".

PAPER PIECING THE BLOCKS

Photocopy 9 copies of paper piecing Pattern A and 18 copies of paper piecing Patterns B – F, pages 47 – 49. Follow Paper Piecing, page 52, to paper piece Blocks.

1. Use **Pattern A** and blue print for areas 1 and 3 and pink print for area 2 to make **Unit 1**. Make 9 **Unit 1's**.
2. Use **Pattern B** and green print for areas 1 and 3 and blue print for area 2 to make **Unit 2**. Make 18 **Unit 2's**.
3. Use **Pattern C** and blue print for area 1, cream polka dot for area 2, and pink print for area 3 to make **Unit 3**. Make 18 **Unit 3's**.
4. Use **Pattern D** and blue print for area 1 and cream polka dot for area 2 to make **Unit 4**. Make 18 **Unit 4's**.
5. Use **Pattern E** and cream polka dot for areas 1 and 3, blue print for area 2, and pink print for area 4 to make **Unit 5**. Make 18 **Unit 5's**.
6. Use **Pattern F** and blue print for area 1 and cream polka dot for areas 2 and 3 to make **Unit 6**. Make 18 **Unit 6's**.
7. Sew 1 **Unit 1** and 2 **Unit 2's** together to make **Unit 7**. Make 9 **Unit 7's**.
8. Sew 1 **Unit 3** and 1 **Unit 4** together to make **Unit 8**. Make 18 **Unit 8's**.
9. Sew 1 **Unit 5** and 1 **Unit 6** together to make **Unit 9**. Make 18 **Unit 9's**.

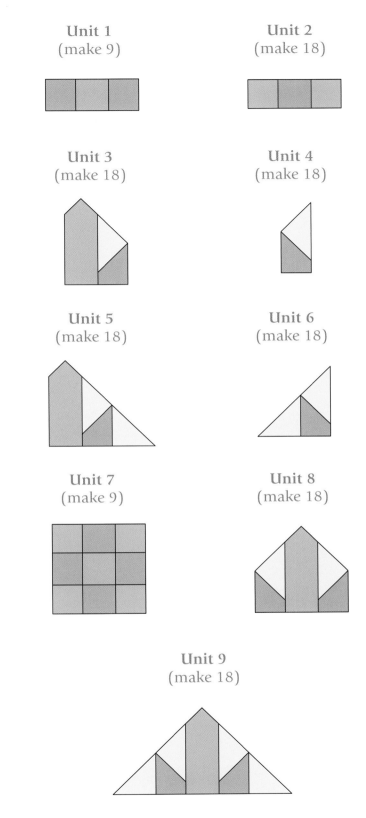

Unit 1
(make 9)

Unit 2
(make 18)

Unit 3
(make 18)

Unit 4
(make 18)

Unit 5
(make 18)

Unit 6
(make 18)

Unit 7
(make 9)

Unit 8
(make 18)

Unit 9
(make 18)

"Grace looked down at the quilt at her fingertips. Shining Hour was a traditional pattern. A nine-patch block, on point like a diamond, adorned the center of an eight-point star, with longer ribbon-like strips extending outward to connect the star to its neighbors, so that the effect was like an elaborately woven tapestry."

—from Sister's Choice

Unit 10
(make 9)

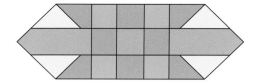

Shining Hour Block
(make 9)

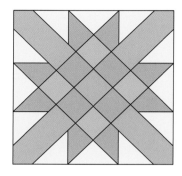

Fig. 1   **Fig. 2**   **Fig. 3**

Unit 11
(make 20 pink and 8 green)

Fig. 4   **Triangle-Squares**
                        (make 28)

10. Sew 1 **Unit 7** and 2 **Unit 8's** together to make **Unit 10**. Make 9 **Unit 10's**.

11. Sew 1 **Unit 10** and 2 **Unit 9's** together to make **Shining Hour Block**. Make 9 **Shining Hour Blocks**. Carefully remove paper from **Blocks**.

ASSEMBLING THE QUILT TOP CENTER

Follow Piecing, page 51, and Pressing, page 53. Use 1/4" seam allowances throughout. Refer to Quilt Top Diagram, page 46, for placement.

1. Sew 3 **Shining Hour Blocks** together to make **Row**. Make 3 **Rows**.

2. Sew **Rows** together to make **Quilt Top Center**.

MAKING THE PIECED BORDER

1. Draw diagonal line (corner to corner) on wrong side of each cream polka dot **small square** and each cream polka dot **large square**.

2. With right sides together, place 1 cream polka dot **small square** on 1 corner of 1 pink print **medium square** and stitch along drawn line (**Fig. 1**). Trim 1/4" from stitching line (**Fig. 2**). Open up and press (**Fig. 3**).

3. Continue adding cream polka dot **small squares** to corners of **medium square**. Open up and press to make **Unit 11**. Make 20 pink **Unit 11's** and 8 green **Unit 11's**.

4. With right sides together, place 1 cream polka dot **large square** on top of 1 blue print **large square**. Stitch seam 1/4" from each side of drawn line (**Fig. 4**).

5. Cut along drawn line and press open to make 2 **Triangle-Squares**. Make 28 **Triangle-Squares**.

6. On wrong side of 14 **Triangle-Squares**, draw diagonal line (corner to corner and perpendicular to seam).

7. Place 1 marked **Triangle-Square** on top of 1 unmarked **Triangle-Square** with like prints opposite each other. Stitch $1/4$" from each side of drawn line (**Fig. 5**). Cut apart along drawn line; press open to make 2 **Hourglasses**. Make 28 **Hourglasses**.

8. Sew 7 **Hourglasses**, 2 green **Unit 11's**, and 4 pink **Unit 11's** together to make **side pieced borders**. Make 2 **side pieced borders**. Set **borders** aside.

9. Sew 7 **Hourglasses**, 2 green **Unit 11's**, and 6 pink **Unit 11's** together to make **top pieced border**. Repeat to make **bottom pieced border**. Set **borders** aside.

ADDING THE BORDERS

1. Matching centers and corners, sew **side inner borders** to **Quilt Top Center**.

2. Matching centers and corners, sew **top/ bottom inner borders** to **Quilt Top**.

3. Follow Steps 1 – 2 to sew **pieced borders** and **outer borders** to **Quilt Top**.

Fig. 5

Hourglass (make 28)

Side Pieced Borders (make 2)

Top/Bottom Pieced Borders (make 2)

COMPLETING THE QUILT

1. Follow **Quilting**, page 54, to mark, layer, and quilt as desired. Our quilt is machine quilted with outline quilting around the pink areas of the blocks and squares in the pieced border. The nine patches and "star points" in the blocks and hour glasses in the pieced border are quilted in-the-ditch and all of the cream areas are meander quilted.
2. Follow **Making a Hanging Sleeve**, page 59, if a hanging sleeve is desired.
3. Follow **Binding**, page 60, and use **binding strips** and to bind quilt.

Quilt Top Diagram

"Grace had wanted Jamie to think of spring and hope whenever she snuggled under the quilt. She thought of this as a comfort quilt, lap size and lightweight, for Jamie to carry with her."

—from Sister's Choice

	Pattern A	
3	**2**	**1**

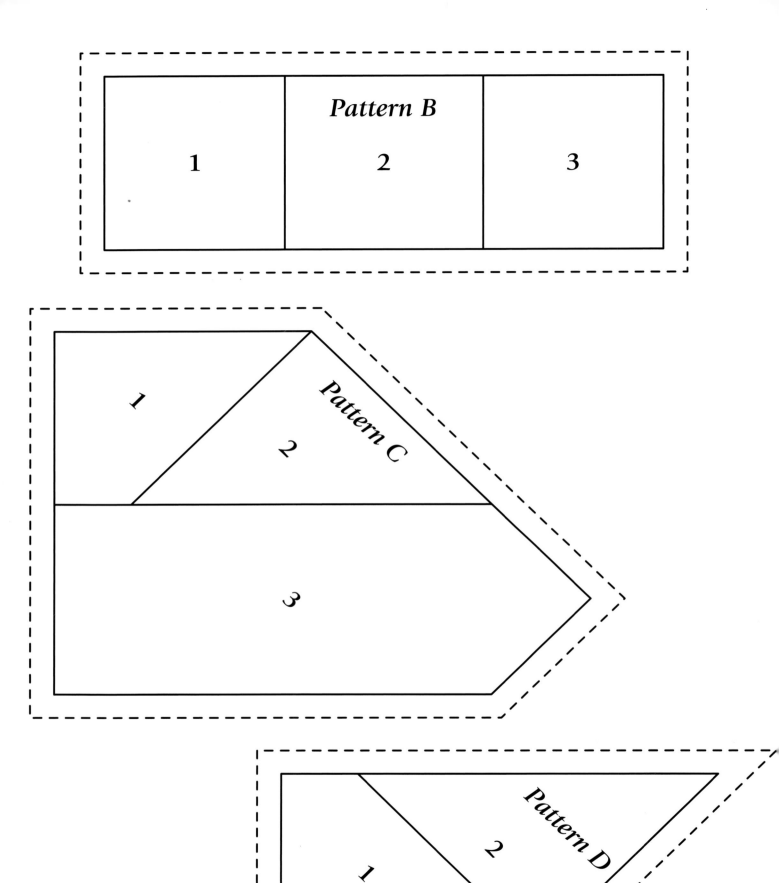

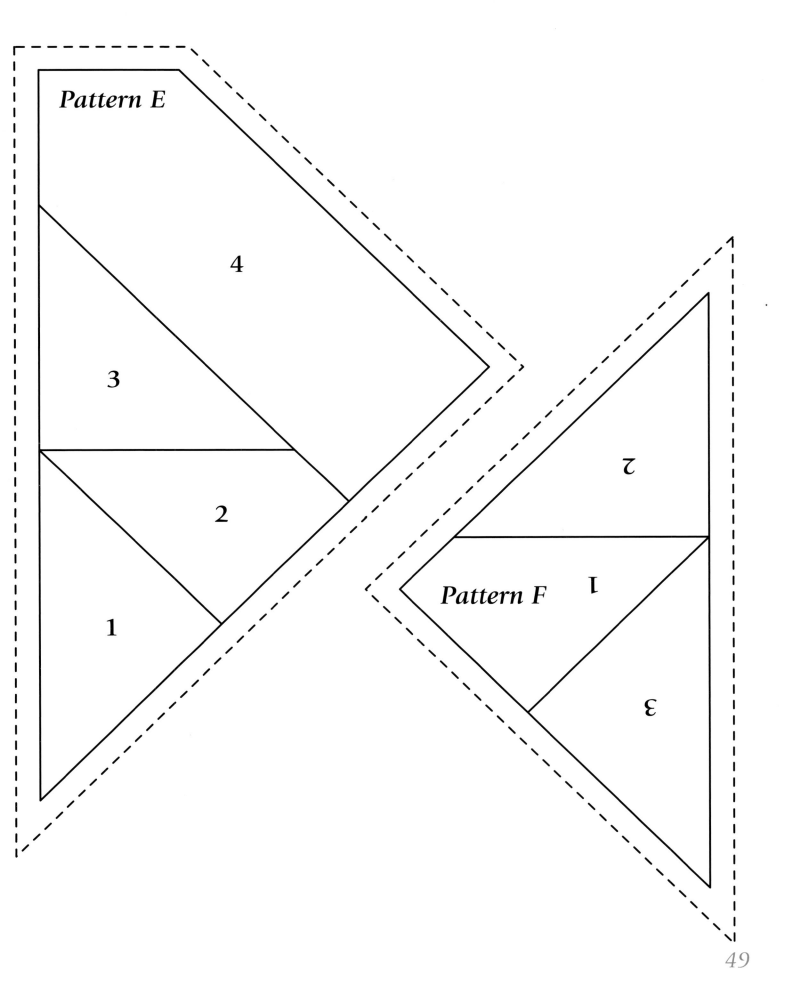

Pattern E

4

3

2

1

Pattern F

1

2

3

49

General Instructions

To make your quilting easier and more enjoyable, we encourage you to carefully read all of the general instructions, study the color photographs, and familiarize yourself with the individual project instructions before beginning a project.

Fig. 1

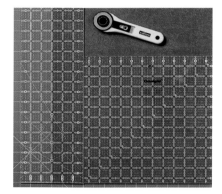

Fig. 2

Fig. 3

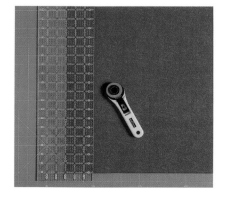

FABRICS

SELECTING FABRICS

Choose high-quality, medium-weight 100% cotton fabrics. All-cotton fabrics hold a crease better, fray less, and are easier to quilt than cotton/polyester blends.

Yardage requirements listed for each project are based on 43"/44" wide fabric with a "usable" width of 40" after shrinkage and trimming selvages. Actual usable width will probably vary slightly from fabric to fabric. Our recommended yardage lengths should be adequate for occasional re-squaring of fabric when many cuts are required.

PREPARING FABRICS

We recommend that all fabrics be washed, dried, and pressed before cutting. If fabrics are not pre-washed, washing the finished quilt will cause shrinkage and give it a more "antiqued" look and feel. Bright and dark colors, which may run, should always be washed before cutting. After washing and drying fabric, fold lengthwise with wrong sides together and matching selvages.

ROTARY CUTTING

Rotary cutting has brought speed and accuracy to quiltmaking by allowing quilters to easily cut strips of fabric and then cut those strips into smaller pieces.

- Place fabric on work surface with fold closest to you.

- Cut all strips from the selvage-to-selvage width of the fabric unless otherwise indicated in project instructions.

- Square left edge of fabric using rotary cutter and rulers (**Figs. 1 - 2**).

- To cut each strip required for a project, place ruler over cut edge of fabric, aligning desired marking on ruler with cut edge (**Fig. 3**); make cut.

- When cutting several strips from a single piece of fabric, it is important to make sure that cuts remain at a perfect right angle to the fold; square fabric as needed.

TEMPLATE CUTTING

Our piecing template patterns have two lines – a solid cutting line and a dashed line showing the $1/4$" seam allowance. Patterns for appliqué templates do not include seam allowances.

1. To make a template from a pattern, use a permanent fine-point pen and a ruler (for straight lines) to carefully trace pattern onto template plastic, making sure to transfer any alignment and grain line markings. Cut out template along inner edge of drawn line. Check template against original pattern for accuracy.

2. To use a piecing template, place template face down on wrong side of fabric, aligning grain line on template with straight grain of fabric. Use a sharp fabric-marking pencil to draw around template. Cut out fabric piece using scissors or rotary cutting equipment.

3. To use appliqué templates, place template face up on right side of fabric. Use a mechanical pencil with a very fine lead to lightly draw around template on fabric. Leaving at least 1" between shapes, repeat for number of shapes specified in project instructions. Use scissors to cut out appliqués approximately $3/16$" outside drawn line.

PIECING

Precise cutting, followed by accurate piecing, will ensure that all pieces of quilt top fit together well.

- Set sewing machine stitch length for approximately 11 stitches per inch.

- Use neutral-colored general-purpose sewing thread (not quilting thread) in needle and in bobbin.

- An accurate $1/4$" seam allowance is *essential*. Presser feet that are $1/4$" wide are available for most sewing machines.

- When piecing, always place pieces right sides together and match raw edges; pin if necessary.

- Chain piecing saves time and will usually result in more accurate piecing.

- Trim away points of seam allowances that extend beyond edges of sewn pieces.

"Jamie followed her children to Grace's kitchen, admiring what looked like primitive antiques but were probably long-held family pieces. And everywhere she looked there were quilts. Not the old-fashioned quilts Jamie had investigated in the surrounding towns at antique and craft shops, but quilts like none Jamie had ever seen."

—from Sister's Choice

Fig. 4

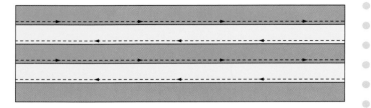

Fig. 5

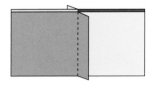

Fig. 6

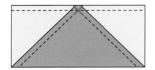

Fig. 7   **Fig. 8**

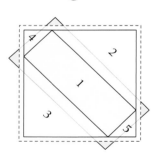   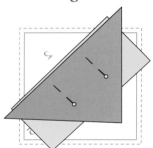

SEWING STRIP SETS

When there are several strips to assemble into a strip set, first sew strips together into pairs, then sew pairs together to form strip set. To help avoid distortion, sew seams in opposite directions (**Fig. 4**).

SEWING ACROSS SEAM INTERSECTIONS

When sewing across intersection of two seams, place pieces right sides together and match seams exactly, making sure seam allowances are pressed in opposite directions (**Fig. 5**).

SEWING SHARP POINTS

To ensure sharp points when joining triangular or diagonal pieces, stitch across the center of the "X" (shown in pink) formed on wrong side by previous seams (**Fig. 6**).

PAPER PIECING

Very important: Shorten stitch length to 18 stitches per inch to make paper removal easier.

*Always stitch seams with the paper foundation on top, right side up. Once a Unit or Block is paper pieced, the pattern and fabric pieces will be **wrong sides together**.*

As you press, use a dry iron (steam will curl the paper). **Note:** *Some photocopied patterns may smear when ironed. Test your patterns and use a pressing cloth if needed.*

1. Rough cut a piece of fabric for area 1 at least $^1/_2$" larger on all sides than area 1 on foundation. With wrong sides together, cover area 1 of foundation with fabric piece for area 1. Pin or glue (using a small dab from a glue stick) fabric in place (**Fig. 7**).
2. Rough cut a piece of fabric for area 2 at least $^1/_2$" larger on all sides than area 2 on foundation. Matching right sides of fabric pieces for areas 1 and 2 and having at least $^1/_4$" of fabric piece for area 2 extending into area 2, pin fabric layers together (**Fig. 8**).

3. With right side of foundation facing up, sew along line between areas 1 and 2, extending sewing a few stitches beyond beginning and ending of line (**Fig. 9**).
4. Fold foundation back on stitched line, and trim seam allowance of fabrics to 1/4" (**Fig. 10**).
5. Open out fabric piece for area 2, press, and pin to foundation (**Fig. 11**).
6. Continue adding pieces in same manner in numerical order until foundation is covered.
7. Trim fabric and foundation along outer dashed lines to complete Unit or Block.
8. When sewing 2 paper pieced Units or Blocks together, align edges by sticking pins straight through patterns at corners and seam intersections (**Fig. 12**). Pin as usual and remove alignment pins. Stitch on seamline, extending stitches to raw edges. Carefully remove paper in seam allowance outside stitching; press seam allowances open.

PRESSING

- Use steam iron set on "Cotton" for all pressing.

- Press after sewing each seam.

- Seam allowances are almost always pressed to one side, usually toward darker fabric. However, to reduce bulk it may occasionally be necessary to press seam allowances toward the lighter fabric or even to press them open.

- To prevent dark fabric seam allowance from showing through light fabric, trim darker seam allowance slightly narrower than lighter seam allowance.

- To press long seams, such as those in long strip sets, without curving or other distortion, lay strips across width of the ironing board.

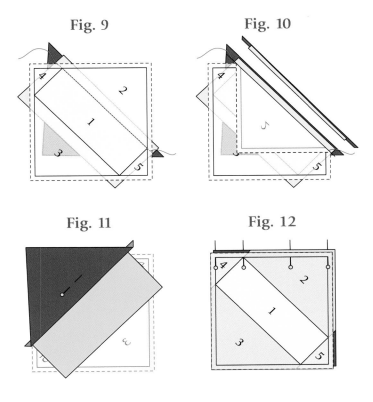

Fig. 9   Fig. 10

Fig. 11   Fig. 12

"'I want you to see my sewing room,' Grace said.

They were wending their way through the house now, heading up the stairs. Grace turned right and went to the end of the hallway, then into the last room. It was large and airy, with cross ventilation and good light. One entire wall was crisscrossed by built-in shelves and cubbyholes filled with rolled-up fabric and what looked to Jamie like quilt batting. Pegboard covered another wall, with lots of things Jamie recognized, such as scissors and rulers, and many more she didn't, hanging from hooks."

—from Sister's Choice

Fig. 13

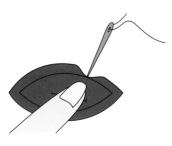

Fig. 14

Fig. 15

Fig. 16

Fig. 17

NEEDLE-TURN APPLIQUÉ

Using a needle to turn under the seam allowance while blindstitching an appliqué to background fabric is called "needle-turn appliqué."

1.   Arrange shapes on background fabric and pin or baste in place.
2.   Thread a sharps needle with a single strand of general-purpose sewing thread that matches appliqué; knot one end.
3.   Begin blindstitching (page 62) on as straight an edge as possible, turning a small section of seam allowance to wrong side with needle, concealing drawn line (**Fig. 13**).
4.   To stitch outward points, stitch to $1/2$" from point (**Fig. 14**). Turn seam allowance under at point (**Fig. 15**); then turn remainder of seam allowance between stitching and point. Stitch to point, taking two or three stitches at top of point to secure. Turn under small amount of seam allowance past point and resume stitching.
5.   To stitch inward point, stitch to $1/2$" from point (**Fig. 16**). Clip to but not through seam allowance at point (**Fig. 17**). Turn seam allowance under between stitching and point. Stitch to point, taking two or three stitches at point to secure. Turn under small amount of seam allowance past point and resume stitching.
6.   Do not turn under or stitch seam allowances that will be covered by other appliqué pieces.
7.   To appliqué pressed bias strips, baste strips in place and blindstitch along edges.
8.   To reduce bulk, background fabric behind appliqués may be cut away. After stitching appliqués in place, turn block over and use sharp scissors or specially designed appliqué scissors to trim away background fabric approximately $3/16$" from stitching line. Take care not to cut appliqué fabric or stitches.

QUILTING

*Quilting holds the three layers (top, batting, and backing) of the quilt together and can be done by hand or machine. Because marking, layering, and quilting are interrelated and may be done in different orders depending on circumstances, please read entire **Quilting** section, pages 54 – 58, before beginning project.*

TYPES OF QUILTING DESIGNS
In the Ditch Quilting
Quilting along seamlines or along edges of appliquéd pieces is called "in the ditch" quilting. This type of quilting should be done on side **opposite** seam allowance and does not have to be marked.

Outline Quilting

Quilting a consistent distance, usually $1/4$", from seam or appliqué is called "outline" quilting. Outline quilting may be marked, or $1/4$" masking tape may be placed along seamlines for quilting guide. (Do not leave tape on quilt longer than necessary, since it may leave an adhesive residue.)

Motif Quilting

Quilting a design, such as a feathered wreath, is called "motif" quilting. This type of quilting should be marked before basting quilt layers together.

Echo Quilting

Quilting that follows the outline of an appliquéd or pieced design with two or more parallel lines is called "echo" quilting. This type of quilting does not need to be marked.

Channel Quilting

Quilting with straight, parallel lines is called "channel" quilting. This type of quilting may be marked or stitched using a guide.

Crosshatch Quilting

Quilting straight lines in a grid pattern is called "crosshatch" quilting. Lines may be stitched parallel to edges of quilt or stitched diagonally. This type of quilting may be marked or stitched using a guide.

Meandering Quilting

Quilting in random curved lines and swirls is called "meandering" quilting. Quilting lines should not cross or touch each other. This type of quilting does not need to be marked.

Stipple Quilting

Meandering quilting that is very closely spaced is called "stipple" quilting. Stippling will flatten the area quilted and is often stitched in background areas to raise appliquéd or pieced designs. This type of quilting does not need to be marked.

MARKING QUILTING LINES

Quilting lines may be marked using fabric marking pencils, chalk markers, or water- or air-soluble pens.

Simple quilting designs may be marked with chalk or chalk pencil after basting. A small area may be marked, then quilted, before moving to next area to be marked. Intricate designs should be marked before basting using a more durable marker.

Caution: Pressing may permanently set some marks. **Test** different markers **on scrap fabric** to find one that marks clearly and can be thoroughly removed.

"'I wish I had time to work with my hands,' Jamie said. 'I've always wanted to do something. Knit, crochet, paint.'

'Be careful what you wish for, and keep your voice down,' Kendra replied.

Jamie turned. 'What? Who's listening?'

Kendra lowered her voice. 'The quilters.'

'Quilters?'

'Now you've gone and done it. They'll be here momentarily. Toms Brook is crawling with them.'"

—from Sister's Choice

Fig. 18

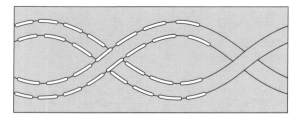

Fig. 19

Fig. 20

Fig. 21

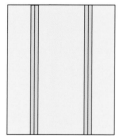

A wide variety of pre-cut quilting stencils, as well as entire books of quilting patterns, are available. Using a stencil makes it easier to mark intricate or repetitive designs.

To make a stencil from a pattern, center template plastic over pattern and use a permanent marker to trace pattern onto plastic. Use a craft knife with single or double blade to cut channels along traced lines (**Fig. 18**).

PREPARING THE BACKING

To allow for slight shifting of quilt top during quilting, backing should be approximately 4" larger on all sides (2" larger on all sides for small quilts). Yardage requirements listed for quilt backings are calculated for 43"/44"w fabric. Using 90"w or 108"w fabric for the backing of a bed-sized quilt may eliminate piecing. To piece a backing using 43"/44"w fabric, use the following instructions.

1. Measure length and width of quilt top; add 8" (4") to each measurement.
2. If determined width is 79" or less, cut backing fabric into two lengths the determined *length* measurement. Trim selvages. Place lengths with right sides facing and sew long edges together, forming tube (**Fig. 19**). Match seams and press along one fold (**Fig. 20**). Cut along pressed fold to form single piece (**Fig. 21**).
3. If determined width is more than 79", divide determined *width* measurement by 40" to determine how many widths will be needed. Cut required number of widths the determined *length* measurement. Trim selvages. Sew long edges together to form single piece.
4. Trim backing to size determined in Step 1; press seam allowances open.

CHOOSING THE BATTING

The appropriate batting will make quilting easier. For fine hand quilting, choose low-loft batting. All cotton or cotton/polyester blend battings work well for machine quilting because the cotton helps "grip" quilt layers. If quilt is to be tied, a high-loft batting, sometimes called extra-loft or fat batting, may be used to make quilt "fluffy."

Types of batting include cotton, polyester, wool, cotton/polyester blend, cotton/wool blend, and silk.

When selecting batting, refer to package labels for characteristics and care instructions. Cut batting same size as prepared backing.

ASSEMBLING THE QUILT

1. Examine wrong side of quilt top closely; trim any seam allowances and clip any threads that may show through front of the quilt. Press quilt top, being careful not to "set" any marked quilting lines.
2. Place backing *wrong* side up on flat surface. Use masking tape to tape edges of backing to surface. Place batting on top of backing fabric. Smooth batting gently, being careful not to stretch or tear. Center quilt top *right* side up on batting.
3. If hand quilting, begin in center and work toward outer edges to hand baste all layers together. Use long stitches and place basting lines approximately 4" apart (**Fig. 22**). Smooth fullness or wrinkles toward outer edges.
4. If machine quilting, use 1" rustproof safety pins to "pin-baste" all layers together, spacing pins approximately 4" apart. Begin at center and work toward outer edges to secure all layers. If possible, place pins away from areas that will be quilted, although pins may be removed as needed when quilting.

HAND QUILTING

The quilting stitch is a basic running stitch that forms a broken line on quilt top and backing. Stitches on quilt top and backing should be straight and equal in length.

1. Secure center of quilt in hoop or frame. Check quilt top and backing to make sure they are smooth. To help prevent puckers, always begin quilting in the center of quilt and work toward outside edges.
2. Thread needle with 18" - 20" length of quilting thread; knot one end. Using thimble, insert needle into quilt top and batting approximately 1/2" from quilting line. Bring needle up on quilting line (**Fig. 23**); when knot catches on quilt top, give thread a quick, short pull to "pop" knot through fabric into batting (**Fig. 24**).
3. Holding needle with sewing hand and placing other hand underneath quilt, use thimble to push tip of needle down through all layers. As soon as needle touches finger underneath, use that finger to push tip of needle only back up through layers to top of quilt. (The amount of needle showing above fabric determines length of quilting stitch.) Referring to **Fig. 25**, rock needle up and down, taking three to six stitches before bringing needle and thread completely through layers. Check back of quilt to make sure stitches are going through all layers. If necessary, make one stitch at a time when quilting through seam allowances or along curves and corners.
4. At end of thread, knot thread close to fabric and "pop" knot into batting; clip thread close to fabric.
5. Move hoop as often as necessary. Thread may be left dangling and picked up again after returning to that part of quilt.

Fig. 22

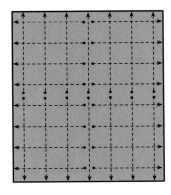

Fig. 23

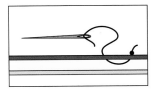

Fig. 24

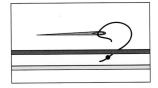

Fig. 25

MACHINE QUILTING METHODS

Use general-purpose thread in bobbin. Do not use quilting thread. Thread the needle of machine with general-purpose thread or transparent monofilament thread to make quilting blend with quilt top fabrics. Use decorative thread, such as a metallic or contrasting-color general-purpose thread, to make quilting lines stand out more.

Straight-Line Quilting

The term "straight-line" is somewhat deceptive, since curves (especially gentle ones) as well as straight lines can be stitched with this technique.

1. Set stitch length for six to ten stitches per inch and attach walking foot to sewing machine.
2. Determine which section of quilt will have longest continuous quilting line, oftentimes area from center top to center bottom. Roll up and secure each edge of quilt to help reduce the bulk, keeping fabrics smooth. Smaller projects may not need to be rolled.
3. Begin stitching on longest quilting line, using very short stitches for the first 1/4" to "lock" quilting. Stitch across project, using one hand on each side of walking foot to slightly spread fabric and to guide fabric through machine. Lock stitches at end of quilting line.
4. Continue machine quilting, stitching longer quilting lines first to stabilize quilt before moving on to other areas.

Free-Motion Quilting

Free-motion quilting may be free form or may follow a marked pattern.

1. Attach darning foot to sewing machine and lower or cover feed dogs.
2. Position quilt under darning foot; lower foot. Holding top thread, take a stitch and pull bobbin thread to top of quilt. To "lock" beginning of quilting line, hold top and bobbin threads while making three to five stitches in place.
3. Use one hand on each side of darning foot to slightly spread fabric and to move fabric through the machine. Even stitch length is achieved by using smooth, flowing hand motion and steady machine speed. Slow machine speed and fast hand movement will create long stitches. Fast machine speed and slow hand movement will create short stitches. Move quilt sideways, back and forth, in a circular motion, or in a random motion to create desired designs; do not rotate quilt. Lock stitches at end of each quilting line.

TYING A QUILT

Tied quilts use pearl cotton, embroidery floss, yarn, or ribbon ties instead of quilting stitches to secure the layers. You may choose a higher loft batting when tying.

1. Layer backing (right side down), batting, and quilt top (right side up). Pin layers together with safety pins or stretch on a quilting frame.
2. Thread a large darning needle with approximately 18" (46 cm) of thread, yarn, or ribbon; do not knot.
3. At each corner between blocks, take a small stitch through all layers of quilt. Pull up thread and tie using a square knot. Clip ends to desired length (ours are 1").

MAKING A HANGING SLEEVE

Attaching a hanging sleeve to back of wall hanging or quilt before the binding is added allows project to be displayed on a wall.

1. Measure width of quilt top edge and subtract 1". Cut piece of fabric 7"w by determined measurement.
2. Press short edges of fabric piece $1/4$" to wrong side; press edges $1/4$" to wrong side again and machine stitch in place.
3. Matching wrong sides, fold piece in half lengthwise to form tube.
4. Follow project instructions to sew binding to quilt top and to trim backing and batting. Before Blindstitching binding to backing, match raw edges and stitch hanging sleeve to center top edge on back of quilt.
5. Finish binding quilt, treating hanging sleeve as part of backing.
6. Blindstitch (page 62) bottom of hanging sleeve to backing, taking care not to stitch through to front of quilt.
7. Insert dowel or slat into hanging sleeve.

MAKING A CONTINUOUS BIAS STRIP

Bias strips for appliquéing can simply be cut and pieced to desired length. However, when a long length of bias strip is needed, the "continuous" method is quick and accurate.

1. Cut square from appliqué fabric the size indicated in project instructions. Cut square in half diagonally to make two triangles.
2. With right sides together and using $1/4$" seam allowance, sew triangles together (**Fig. 26**); press seam allowances open.
3. On wrong side of fabric, draw lines the width of bias strip as specified in project instructions, usually $1^1/4$" (**Fig. 27**). Cut off any remaining fabric less than this width.
4. With right sides inside, bring short edges together to form tube; match raw edges so that first drawn line of top section meets second drawn line of bottom section (**Fig. 28**).
5. Carefully pin edges together by inserting pins through drawn lines at point where drawn lines intersect, making sure pins go through intersections on both sides. Using $1/4$" seam allowance, sew edges together; press seam allowances open.
6. To cut continuous strip, begin cutting along first drawn line (**Fig. 29**). Continue cutting along drawn line around tube.
7. Trim ends of bias strip square.

Fig. 26

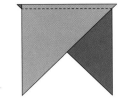

Fig. 27

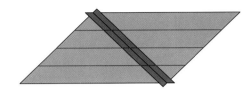

Fig. 28

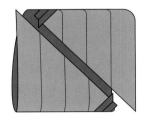

Fig. 29

Fig. 30

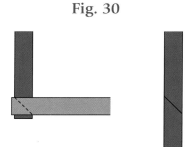

BINDING

1. Matching short ends and using a diagonal seam, sew binding strips called for in project together (**Fig. 30**).

2. Matching wrong sides and raw edges, press strip in half lengthwise to complete binding.

3. Beginning with one end near center on bottom edge of quilt, lay binding around quilt to make sure that seams in binding will not end up at a corner. Adjust placement if necessary. Matching raw edges of binding to raw edge of quilt top, pin binding to right side of quilt along one edge.

4. When you reach first corner, mark $1/4$" from corner of quilt top (**Fig. 31**).

5. Beginning approximately 10" from end of binding and using $1/4$" seam allowance, sew binding to quilt, backstitching at beginning of stitching and at mark (**Fig. 32**). Lift needle out of fabric and clip thread.

6. Fold binding as shown in **Figs. 33 – 34** and pin binding to adjacent side, matching raw edges. When you've reached the next corner, mark $1/4$" from edge of quilt top.

7. Backstitching at edge of quilt top, sew pinned binding to quilt (**Fig. 35**); backstitch at the next mark. Lift needle out of fabric and clip thread.

8. Continue sewing binding to quilt, stopping approximately 10" from starting point (**Fig. 36**).

Fig. 31

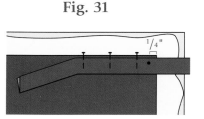

Fig. 32

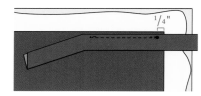

Fig. 33

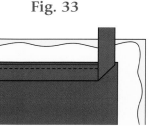

Fig. 34

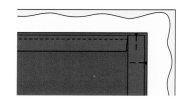

Fig. 35

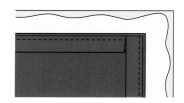

Fig. 36

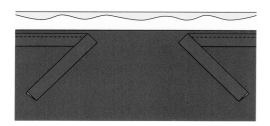

9. Bring beginning and end of binding to center of opening and fold each end back, leaving a $1/4$" space between folds (**Fig. 37**). Finger press folds.

10. Unfold ends of binding and draw a line across wrong side in finger-pressed crease. Draw a line through the lengthwise pressed fold of binding at the same spot to create a cross mark. With edge of ruler at cross mark, line up 45° angle marking on ruler with one long side of binding. Draw a diagonal line from edge to edge. Repeat on remaining end, making sure that the two diagonal lines are angled the same way (**Fig. 38**).

11. Matching right sides and diagonal lines, pin binding ends together at right angles (**Fig. 39**).

12. Machine stitch along diagonal line (**Fig. 40**), removing pins as you stitch.

13. Lay binding against quilt to double check that it is correct length.

14. Trim binding ends, leaving $1/4$" seam allowance; press seam open. Stitch binding to quilt.

15. Trim backing and batting even with edges of quilt top.

16. On one edge of quilt, fold binding over to quilt backing and pin pressed edge in place, covering stitching line (**Fig. 41**). On adjacent side, fold binding over, forming a mitered corner (**Fig. 42**). Repeat to pin remainder of binding in place.

17. Blindstitch (page 62) binding to backing, taking care not to stitch through to front of quilt.

"'Do you have a quilt in progress,' Jamie asked. 'Yes, indeed,' Grace replied. 'That's a question you never have to ask a quilter. There are quilts in our heads, quilts in the way we pile fabrics on our shelves, quilts on our design walls, under the needles in our sewing machines. Quilts waiting to be bound. Always quilts. Some of us will die planning the next one. We won't even notice that final breath.'"

—from Sister's Choice

Fig. 37

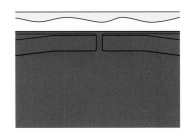

Fig. 38

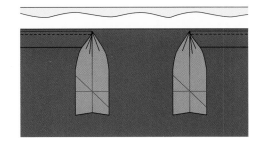

Fig. 39

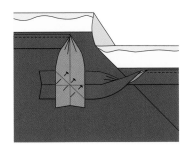

Fig. 40

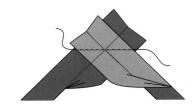

Fig. 41   **Fig. 42**

HAND STITCHES

Backstitch

Blanket Stitch

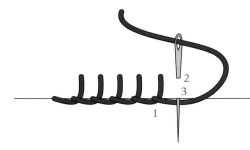

Blanket Variation Stitch

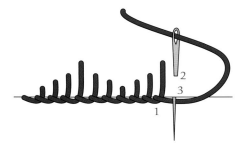

Blindstitch

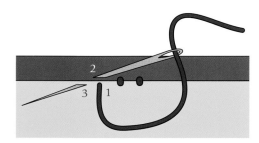

Buttonhole Wheel

Chain Stitch

Chevron Stitch

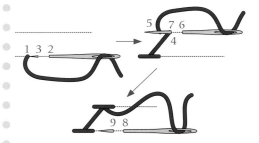

Closed Cretan Stitch

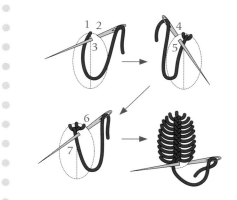

Couching

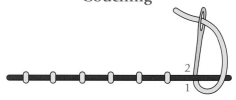

Cretan Stitch

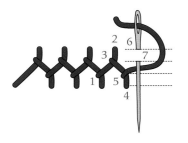

Cross Stitch

Cross Stitch Variation Star

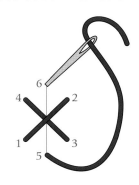

Double Cross Stitch

Feather Stitch

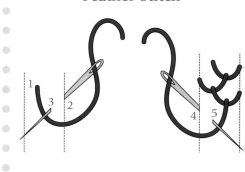

Fishbone Stitch

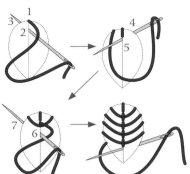

Fly Stitch

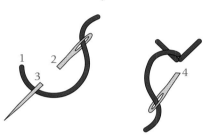

French Knot

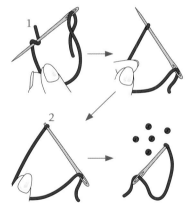

Herringbone Stitch

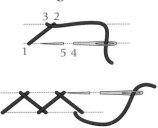

Lazy Daisy Stitch

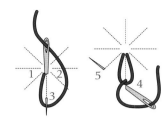

Running Stitch

Satin Stitch

Stem Stitch

Straight Stitch

"'Oh, no wonder you do this.' Jamie was entranced. Grace was clearly in the process of cutting fabric for another quilt. A high table was covered by a large rectangle in a bold floral print."

—from Sister's Choice

Many thanks go to these ladies for their beautiful work.

Snake in the Hollow Quilt

was pieced and bound by Nelwyn Gray
and quilted by Julie Schrader

Alison's First Quilt

was pieced and tied by Jean Lewis
and bound by Larcie Burnett

Sister's Choice Quilt

was pieced by Larcie Burnett,
quilted by Julie Schrader,
and bound by Diane Fischer

the alternate color way
was pieced by Lisa Lancaster,
quilted by Julie Schrader,
and bound by Diane Fischer

Bear's Paw Quilt

was embroidered by Diane Fischer,
pieced by Larcie Burnett and Nelwyn Gray,
and quilted and bound by Nelwyn Gray

Crazy Cats Quilt

was pieced by Nelwyn Gray,
embroidered by Donna Overman,
and tied and bound by Larcie Burnett

Quilt inspired by an original design by Patricia Eaton.

Shining Hour Quilt

was pieced by Larcie Burnett,
quilted by Julie Schrader,
and bound by Lisa Lancaster

EDITORIAL STAFF
Executive Publications Director: Susan White Sullivan
Designer Relations Director: Debra Nettles
Quilt Publications Director: Cheryl Johnson
Special Projects Director: Susan Frantz Wiles
Senior Prepress Director: Mark Hawkins
Technical Editor: Lisa Lancaster
Technical Writer: Frances Huddleston
Editorial Writer: Susan McManus Johnson
Staff Designers: Lisa Lancaster, Jean Lewis, Anne Stocks, and
    Frances Huddleston
Art Publications Director: Rhonda Shelby
Art Category Manager: Lora Puls
Graphic Artist: Amy Temple
Imaging Technicians: Brian Hall, Stephanie Johnson,
    and Mark R. Potter
Photography Manager: Katherine Atchison
Photography Stylist: Christy Myers
Photographer: Mark Mathews
Publishing Systems Administrator: Becky Riddle
Publishing Systems Assistants: Clint Hanson
    and John Rose

BUSINESS STAFF
Vice President and Chief Operations Officer:
    Tom Siebenmorgen
Corporate Planning and Development Director:
    Laticia Mull Dittrich
Vice President, Sales and Marketing: Pam Stebbins
National Accounts Director: Martha Adams
Sales and Services Director: Margaret Reinold
Vice President, Operations: Jim Dittrich
Comptroller, Operations: Rob Thieme
Retail Customer Service Manager: Stan Raynor
Print Production Manager: Fred F. Pruss

ISBN 10: 1-60140-868-4
ISBN 13: 978-1-60140-868-6